GREEN TRANSPORTATION

T0008896

Priyanka Lamichhane

Children's Press®
An imprint of Scholastic Inc.

Content Consultant
Jeslin Varghese, LEED AP, WELL AP
President & Director of Sustainability
GBRI

To Leah Lakshmi, Emma Arya, and Jonah Jai, my loves. How lucky I am to be your mom.
—Priyanka Lamichhane

Library of Congress Cataloging-in-Publication Data
Names: Lamichhane, Priyanka, author.
Title: Green transportation / Priyanka Lamichhane.
Description: First edition. | New York : Children's Press, an imprint of Scholastic Inc. 2024. | Series: A true book: a green future | Includes bibliographical references and index. | Audience: Ages 8–10. | Audience: Grades 3–5. | Summary: "This STEM-based set of True Books introduces students to the engineering innovations that can help us reach more environmentally friendly goals"— Provided by publisher.
Identifiers: LCCN 2023019130 (print) | LCCN 2023019131 (ebook) | ISBN 9781339020815 (library binding) | ISBN 9781339020822 (paperback) | ISBN 9781339020839 (ebk)
Subjects: LCSH: Transportation—Environmental aspects—Juvenile literature. | Vehicles—Motors—Exhaust gas—Environmental aspects—Juvenile literature. | BISAC: JUVENILE NONFICTION / Science & Nature / Environmental Conservation & Protection | JUVENILE NONFICTION / Science & Nature / Earth Sciences / General
Classification: LCC HE152 .L335 2024 (print) | LCC HE152 (ebook) | DDC 388.3028/6—dc23/eng/20230426
LC record available at https://lccn.loc.gov/2023019130
LC ebook record available at https://lccn.loc.gov/2023019131

10 9 8 7 6 5 4 3 2 1   24 25 26 27 28

Printed in China 62
First edition, 2024

Design by Kathleen Petelinsek
Series produced by Spooky Cheetah Press

Front cover: SolarWorld's solar-powered race car

Find the Truth!

Everything you are about to read is true *except* for one of the sentences on this page.

Which one is **TRUE**?

T or F Riding on a train is better for the environment than riding on a bus.

T or F The first mass-produced electric vehicle was introduced in 2017.

Find the answers in this book.

What's in This Book?

The **BIG** Truth

The first
electric car
was released
in 1902.

The Battery Dilemma

Tesla's Cybertruck is an electric pickup truck.

3 Green Vehicles on the Water

How can we reduce pollution caused by boats and ships?

4 Green Vehicles in the Air

Are environmentally friendly planes, helicopters, and rockets possible?

The future of spaceflight is green!

INTRODUCTION

It takes a **lot of energy** to **power the vehicles** that we rely on every day—and **fossil fuels** are the most common source of that energy. Fossil fuels are made from the remains of living things—like plants and animals—that died long ago. **Oil**, **coal**, and **natural gas** are all fossil fuels. They are nonrenewable forms of energy, which means that one day **they will run out**. Burning fossil fuels is also bad for our planet. When we burn oil, coal, or gas, heat-trapping **greenhouse gases** like carbon dioxide (CO_2) are released into the atmosphere. An increase in these gases in our atmosphere has caused a rise in Earth's surface temperature. This is called **global warming**, and it contributes to **climate change**.

Greenhouse gases trap heat in Earth's atmosphere. Human activity has increased the amount of these gases to record highs.

Globally, there are more than one billion vehicles on the roads.

The **future is looking brighter**, though. People are working to reduce their **carbon footprint**. That is the amount of greenhouse gases that are generated from our actions, including buying clothes, eating, and traveling. Experts around the world have been working for years to manufacture vehicles with smaller **carbon footprints**. That is where green vehicles come in!

Vehicles are now made with more efficient designs, which means they can go farther using less fuel. And the **technologies** used to power engines have **gotten cleaner** too. Some vehicles **run on electricity**. Others use **alternative fuels** like **hydrogen** and **biofuels**. All these vehicles require **less energy to run** and **produce less pollution**. This is why they are better for our planet. Read on to learn how the **future of transportation is green!**

Wind power is clean energy. So is the hydrogen-fuel technology used by this BMW iX5.

In the United States, transportation accounts for about 30 percent of energy consumption.

More than 74 percent of cars on the roads in Norway are electric. That's more than any other country.

The Mercedes-AMG EQS 53 runs on electricity instead of gas.

Green Vehicles on the Road

Gas-powered passenger vehicles, such as motorcycles, cars, SUVs, and pickup trucks, are not only noisy, but they are also some of the biggest greenhouse gas contributors on the planet. And the **exhaust** created from burning fossil fuels causes air pollution. Making vehicles that run on the road more fuel efficient is a huge step forward in helping to slow climate change. Improvements to the way vehicles are built, and the types of engines and fuel they use all help to reduce the amount of gas used for every mile driven.

A Two-Wheeler Revolution

Plug-in two-wheelers, such as motorcycles and scooters, use rechargeable electric batteries instead of fossil fuels. They are very quiet, so they create little noise pollution. Electric two-wheelers don't create any exhaust, so they don't add to air pollution either—while they are being driven. However, electric batteries are not perfect and can cause several problems for the environment. Learn more about that in "The Big Truth" (pages 26–27)!

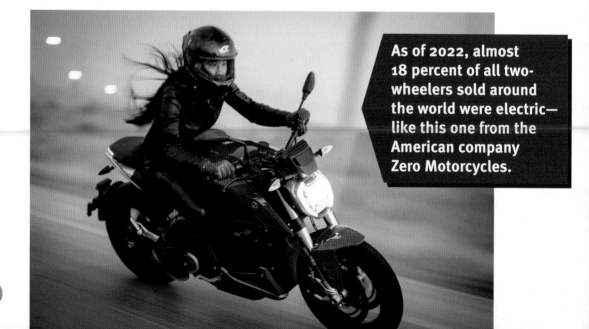

As of 2022, almost 18 percent of all two-wheelers sold around the world were electric—like this one from the American company Zero Motorcycles.

Wildlife Crossings

Roads are laid in places that are convenient for people. But they are often inconvenient—and even deadly—for animals. Collisions with vehicles kill more than 500 million animals every year in Europe and the United States alone. Wildlife crossings, also called "green bridges," can help. These bridges are built over or under highways and are made to become part of the animals' habitat. For that to happen, the type of structure and the placement of the crossing have to be just right. For example, the crossings are covered with plants that make them look like part of the landscape rather than part of the roadway.

This is one of many wildlife crossings on the Trans-Canada Highway.

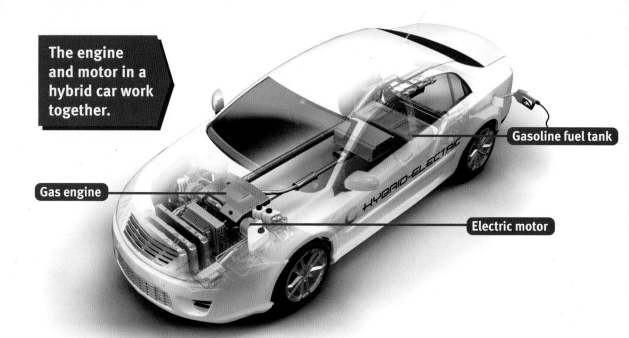

The engine and motor in a hybrid car work together.

Gasoline fuel tank

Gas engine

Electric motor

HYBRID-ELECTRIC

Two Ways to Go

Hybrid vehicles use two types of power to move. They have an engine that runs on gasoline, and they have a motor, connected to a battery, that runs on electricity. When a hybrid car is driving at normal speeds, and each time the car brakes, it charges the car's battery. When the car speeds up, the gas engine gets to work, helping the car go faster. This system helps reduce the amount of gas used so that fewer **emissions** are released into the air.

Getting Better All the Time

The Toyota Prius was the first mass-produced hybrid car in the world. It went on the market in 2000. The Prius could go 41 miles (66 kilometers) on one gallon of gas. Hybrid vehicles have come a long way since then. The 2023 Toyota Prius was able to go 57 miles (92 km) on one gallon. The typical gas-powered car gets only about 30 miles (48 km) to the gallon.

Today there are more than 30 types of hybrid vehicles available from many manufacturers.

The Hyundai Ioniq Blue is a hybrid car that was released in 2016.

Plug and Go

It takes between 4 and 12 hours to fully charge an electric car at a charging station.

An electric car runs completely on electricity. No gas required. The car's motor is powered by a battery. When the battery runs low, the car has to be plugged in to recharge. Like electric two-wheelers, electric cars are very quiet and release zero emissions while being driven, so they are very green.

Timeline: History of Electric Motors

1821
The first electric motor is invented by English chemist Michael Faraday. It uses the voltaic pile battery, which had been invented in 1800 in Italy.

1902
The Studebaker Brothers Manufacturing Company, a wagon-making company, introduces electric cars and trucks. Thomas Edison is one of the first customers.

1982
The U.S. Department of Energy increases its investment in research and development of hybrid and electric vehicles.

1996
General Motors introduces the EV1. It is the first mass-produced electric vehicle. Production stops in 1999.

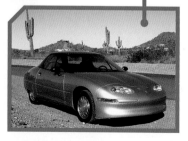

Expanding Their Range

The first fully electric vehicle had about a 50-mile (80-km) range. Today, an electric car can go more than 400 miles (644 km) on a fully charged battery. That's about the distance from Baltimore, Maryland, to New York City! As the technology advances, batteries will become more efficient—and have a lesser impact on the environment.

2000
The Toyota Prius becomes the first mass-produced hybrid vehicle to go on sale to the general public.

2017
The Tesla Model 3 is introduced. In 2019, it overtakes the Nissan Leaf as the best-selling electric vehicle of all time.

2021
Electric car sales in the United States increase from less than 1 percent in 2011 to 3 percent.

2023
Tesla plans to launch the electric Cybertruck. It will be able to go up to 500 miles (805 km) on a single charge.

Trucks Go Green!

Some of today's more eco-friendly **freight** and delivery trucks are electric. Others use biofuels, which are made from plant and animal materials that are burned to create energy. Biofuels are renewable. They won't run out. Burning biofuels does release CO_2. However, when the plants in the biofuels were still alive and growing, they absorbed CO_2. So the CO_2 released is offset by the CO_2 that had previously been absorbed. That makes biofuels **carbon neutral**.

In Toronto, Canada, garbage trucks run on biofuel created from the city's food scraps!

This truck runs on biofuel made from recycled cooking oil. It delivers goods, called freight, all across the country.

The Power of Hydrogen

Other eco-friendly trucks are powered by hydrogen fuel cells. These special motors change hydrogen gas and oxygen into electricity. The only thing released by a hydrogen fuel cell vehicle is pure water! Some passenger cars use this technology too. Vehicles that run on hydrogen fuel cells are carbon neutral.

This electric bus is getting "refueled" at a charging station.

Hop On the Bus

Buses that run on gasoline are harmful to the environment. But even those are better than passenger vehicles. That is because when people use mass transit—like buses—it means there are fewer cars on the road. That means less CO_2 is released into the atmosphere. And, in recent years, many cities and towns have replaced their gas-powered buses with hybrid and electric buses, or those that run on biofuels.

Green Goals

By 2018, more than 50 percent of passenger buses in the United States were hybrid or powered with biofuels. In England, London's famous red double-decker buses are being replaced with electric versions. The city hopes to have an all-electric fleet of double-deckers by 2037. And cities in Mexico, South Africa, and Canada have pledged to buy only electric buses starting in 2025.

As of April 2023, U.S. school districts have more than 5,600 electric school buses operating across the country.

IDO UNION HIGH SCHOOL
APCD

Large batteries power this school bus in California.

Thirty-five percent of the electricity used to power the metro system in New Delhi, India, comes from solar power.

Solar panels turn energy from the sun into electricity for New Delhi's trains.

Green Vehicles on the Rails

Trains and subways are also part of a mass transit system. They even carry more people than buses! This alone makes them a greener option than passenger vehicles and buses. But many trains and subways run on electricity that is often produced using fossil fuels. This harms the environment. Today changes are being made all around the world to operate more **sustainable** trains and subways.

All Aboard!

Most green trains run on hybrid power, electricity, biofuels, or hydrogen fuel cells. Then there is the maglev train. A magnetic guideway repels magnets underneath the train, which causes the train to rise a few inches into the air. Electricity is used to power the guideway, and the train is pulled forward. Because the train is not riding on a track, there is no friction to slow it down—so the train needs even less electricity to move than a regular train.

Going Underground

Subways, or metros, are trains that usually run underground. Subway trains run on a track that provides electricity to the train. Every day, more and more subway systems get electricity from renewable resources like the sun (solar power), the wind (wind power), and moving water (hydroelectric power).

San Francisco is working to make its transit system 100 percent electric. Almost all the electricity comes from green sources like solar and wind power.

The Battery Dilemma

Electric batteries have made it possible for vehicles to stop using fossil fuels to run. They have also reduced levels of noise pollution around the world. But they can still cause problems for our planet. Let's take a look at some of those problems and explore possible solutions.

Electric battery pack

Mining

Problem: Batteries are made with metals such as lithium, cobalt, and nickel. Mining for these metals can destroy the quality of the soil, ruin animal habitats, and pollute waterways. These metals are not renewable, so one day they could run out.

Solution: The batteries can be reused. Then we would not need to mine for more metals when we want to build new batteries.

Cobalt

Lithium

Nickel

Carbon Footprint

Problem: Manufacturing electric car batteries releases a lot of carbon into the atmosphere. Because of this, the carbon footprint of manufacturing an electric vehicle is twice that of manufacturing a gas-powered vehicle.

Solution: In order to reduce carbon emissions, car and battery manufacturers have to work with suppliers that use raw materials that are sustainably extracted and transported. Manufacturers must also use renewable energy in their assembly plants.

Experts are working on ways to make greener batteries.

Pollution

Problem: When old batteries are thrown away, chemicals in the battery can leak out. They pollute the soil and any nearby water.

Solution: The batteries should not be thrown away. If they are not reused, they can be sent to a special facility to be recycled to make new batteries or other products.

Leaky batteries are bad for the planet.

This stadium in Amsterdam, the Netherlands, uses solar power to generate its own electric power. It stores that energy in old electric car batteries.

Ships and other boats account for 3 percent of greenhouse gas emissions.

Huge cargo ships transport goods around the world.

Green Vehicles on the Water

Ships and other boats are some of the planet's biggest polluters. They create air pollution by burning fossil fuels. They cause water pollution when they release dirty, oily wastewater into the seas. As water traffic has increased over the years, the health of our oceans and the marine life that live in them have suffered. But as clean technologies continue to develop, shipping companies have new options for going green.

Super Ships

In the past, a large ship's motor wasn't turned off when it docked at its destination. It was left running to provide electricity to the ship. That is a waste of nonrenewable fuel. It also caused pollution. Today docking stations around the world are allowing ships to plug in to electric power instead. Ships are also installing solar panels and using biofuels and hydrogen fuel cells to power their vessels.

Cruise ships use a lot of energy just to keep the lights on.

An electric ferry in Norway

Going Electric

The Pure Pontoon Boat is an electric fishing boat. It is quiet on the water and runs only on electricity, leaving zero pollutants behind. Electric ferries are becoming more popular too. The world's first electric passenger ferry set sail in Norway in 2015. New York City will soon have electric ferries as well. These boats will run on battery power with a backup hybrid motor.

Clean Cruisers

New eco-ships are also on the horizon. A company called Peace Boat has modeled a low-carbon cruise ship. It has huge solar sails and wind generators that will provide clean, green energy to power these eco-friendly vessels. The ship will carry about 2,000 people and travel all over the world.

Wastewater Clean-Up

Wastewater from cruise ships—which includes laundry water and toilet water—used to be dumped into the sea. Now cruise ships such as Royal Caribbean's *Symphony of the Seas* are cleaning their water before dumping it. Onboard systems take the dirty water from all over the ship and run it through a huge water purification system. The system cleans the water to the point that it is almost good enough to drink. Only then is the clean water released from the ship into the sea.

Glass, cardboard, plastic, and metal are also recycled on board the *Symphony of the Seas.*

About 2.4 percent of all global carbon emissions come from aviation.

Green alternatives in aviation, like this solar plane, are crucial to the health of our planet.

Green Vehicles in the Air

Airplanes, helicopters, and rockets release large amounts of carbon emissions into the air. That's why experts are working on several technologies that will help make air transportation greener and more fuel efficient. The goal of these innovations, known as "green aviation," is for planes, helicopters, and even rockets to use cleaner fuel and travel farther on less.

Flying High

Currently, airlines such as United, British Airways, and Virgin Atlantic all use some amount of biofuel with every flight. In the meantime, scientists and engineers are working on hybrid and fully electric planes—which are not too far from becoming reality. Smaller electric seaplanes are already being tested in Canada. Eco-planes are also being developed and tested to run on solar power or wind power.

The Solar Impulse traveled 25,000 miles (40,000 km) using power generated from the sun!

The Solar Impulse made a test flight around the world in 2016.

The R44 could be the first electric helicopter to deliver organs to hospitals.

Up, Up, and Away

Helicopters emit more than 40 times more pollutants per hour into the air than cars do. Today new helicopters are being developed that will run on clean energy, such as biofuels and electricity. And fully electric helicopters have already taken to the skies. In 2022, the Robinson R44 helicopter became the first electric helicopter to fly 24 miles (39 km). The flight took 20 minutes.

Spacecraft manufacturer SpaceX uses recycled parts to make new rockets and capsules.

Blasting Off

Rockets release huge amounts of jet fuel, smoke, and chemicals into the air at liftoff. Alternative fuels are being tested to help make them greener and cleaner. In fact, in 2002, a NASA launch used super-cold liquid hydrogen to successfully propel a rocket. The only emission was water vapor! There are also companies working to develop "green" rocket fuel that only produces water, nitrogen, and oxygen when heated.

The Future Is Green!

Gas-powered transportation is a major contributor to climate change. But we will be able to slow climate change if the majority of people around the globe commit to green transportation. And then we will all be able to enjoy cleaner air and water, and greener communities.

Fifty-eight percent of passenger cars across the world are expected to be electric by 2040.

Walking is one of the greenest forms of transportation!

A Car of the Future

In 2020, Aptera Motors introduced the world to a car that runs on solar energy. The Aptera solar car, shown here, should be ready to hit the road by the end of 2024. Let's take a look at some of the features that make this a car of the future.

Solar cells gather energy from the sun, which is used to power the car. It can drive up to 40 miles (64 km) a day.

The Aptera is 13 times more efficient than a gas-powered truck and 4 times more efficient than an electric vehicle.

Three wheels instead of four reduces the amount of friction on the tires. That means less energy is needed to move.

The Aptera uses as much energy traveling 1 mile (1.6 km) as a desktop computer uses in 30 minutes.

The aerodynamic shape allows wind to flow easily over and around the car. That reduces the resistance the car faces as it drives and allows it to move using less energy.

A lightweight frame helps with energy efficiency because lighter objects require less energy to move than heavier objects.

An electric power option offers backup power. Some models can go 1,000 miles (1,600 km) on a fully charged battery.

Two people can fit in the Aptera solar car.

Traveling Green

There are lots of easy ways you can make traveling greener. Here are a few ideas.

Use Green Transportation

Look at the transportation pyramid below. Whenever possible, use one of the green forms of transportation shown in the pyramid, such as walking, riding a bike, or using mass transit, instead of riding in a car. No matter which mode of green transportation you use, make sure you are with a trusted grown-up when you are traveling.

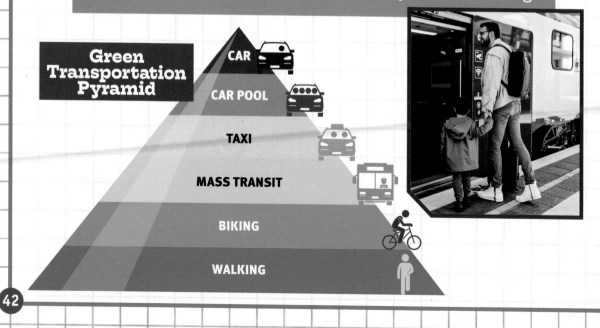

Green Transportation Pyramid

- CAR
- CAR POOL
- TAXI
- MASS TRANSIT
- BIKING
- WALKING

Encourage Others

Talk with your friends and family about the many types of green transportation you learned about in this book. Share with them why it's important to go green when getting around. And encourage them to join you in using green transportation whenever possible.

Advocate for Change

The people who represent us in the government are called politicians. They have a say in what laws are passed, how communities are built, and much more. You can write to your representative to share how important green transportation is to your community. You can help convince them to make changes that are good for our planet. To find out who your representatives are, ask an adult to help you visit official *.gov* websites on the internet.

True Statistics

Percentage of carbon dioxide emissions that come from transportation worldwide: 24

Percentage of greenhouse gas emissions that come from passenger vehicles in the United States: 81

Number of electric vehicles on U.S. roads expected by 2030: over 200 million

Number of electric buses expected to be in use worldwide by 2025: 1.5 million

Gallons of gasoline saved each year in the United States by using public transportation: 6 billion

Number of hydrogen fuel cell trains running in Germany as of 2023: 14

Did you find the truth?

T Riding on a train is better for the environment than riding on a bus.

F The first mass-produced electric vehicle was introduced in 2017.

Resources

Other books in this series:

You can also look at:

Ball, Jacqueline A. *Traveling Green*. New York: Bearport Publishing, 2010.

Eschbach, Christina. *Inside Electric Cars*. Minneapolis: Core Library, 2019.

Peppas, Lynn. *Green Machines: Eco-Friendly Rides*. New York: Crabtree Publishing Company, 2011.

Rebman, Nick. *Earth-Friendly Transportation*. Mendota Heights, MN: North Star Editions, 2021.

Glossary

biofuels (BYE-oh-fyoo-uhlz) fuels that are made from renewable materials such as plants or animal waste

carbon footprint (KAHR-buhn FUT-print) a measure of the amount of carbon dioxide produced by a person, an object, or an organization and released into the atmosphere

carbon neutral (KAHR-buhn NOO-truhl) having or resulting in no net addition of carbon dioxide to the atmosphere

climate change (KLYE-mit CHAYNJ) global warming and other changes in the weather and weather patterns that are happening because of human activity

emissions (i-MISH-uhnz) substances released into the atmosphere

exhaust (ig-ZAWST) the gases or steam produced by the engine of a motor vehicle

fossil fuels (FAH-suhl FYOO-uhlz) coal, oil, or natural gas, formed from the remains of prehistoric plants and animals

freight (FRAYT) goods that are carried by trains, ships, planes, or trucks

greenhouse gases (GREEN-hous GAS-ez) gases such as carbon dioxide and methane that contribute to the greenhouse effect

sustainable (suh-STAY-nuh-buhl) done in a way that can be continued and that doesn't use up natural resources

Index

Page numbers in **bold** indicate illustrations.

About the Author

Priyanka Lamichhane spent 15 years with National Geographic Kids, where she led the reference publishing program and specialized in ideation, content development, editing, and project management. From encyclopedias to guidebooks and atlases to fact books, Priyanka has created hundreds of engaging titles on numerous topics for kids from preschool through middle grade. Most recently, Priyanka has been working with content producers and publishers, using her talents to create engaging books, articles, and activities for children. She loves learning about a wide variety of topics and shares the many fun facts floating around in her head with her three curious kids.

Photos ©: cover: Wally Bauman Photography/Stockimo/Alamy Images; back cover: Noah Berger/AP Images; 3: Amy Osborne/San Francisco Chronicle/AP Images; 4: Courtesy of Classic Auto Mall; 5 Gianrigo Marletta/AFP/Getty Images; 6–7: trekandshoot/Getty Images; 8–9: BMW Group; 10–11: teddyleung/Getty Images; 12: Zero Motorcycles; 13: WikiPedant/Wikimedia; 14: US Department of Energy; 15: Hyundai; 16 left: Design Pics Inc/Shutterstock; 16 center: Courtesy of Classic Auto Mall; 16 right: RightBrainPhotography/Rick Rowen/Wikimedia; 19: Hyundai; 21: Charlie Neuman/ UT San Diego/2014 San Diego Union-Tribune, LLC/ZUMAPRESS.com/Alamy Images; 25: Amy Osborne/San Francisco Chronicle/AP Images; 27 center: Monty Rakusen/Getty Images; 27 bottom: Nicolas Economou/NurPhoto/Shutterstock; 28–29: Art Wager/Getty Images; 30: Maremagnum/Getty Images; 31: Jonathan Sumpton/Alamy Images; 32: Peace Boat; 34–35: Olga Stefatou/Solar Impulse/SIPA/AP Images; 36: Noah Berger/AP Images; 37: Tier 1 Engineering; 38: Gianrigo Marletta/AFP/Getty Images; 40–41 background: billnoll/Getty Images; 40–41 foreground: Aptera.

All other photos © Shutterstock.